THE
NEW REFORMATION CATECHISM ON HUMAN SEXUALITY

*A Catechism Based on
The Heidelberg Catechism of 1563*

Christopher J. Gordon

Published by Gospel Reformation Network & Abounding Grace Radio, 2022

Revised July, 2022

ISBN: 979-8-218-05244-7

www.gospelreformation.net | www.agradio.org

Cover design and layout by Kerri Ann Cruse

© Gospel Reformation Network & Abounding Grace Radio. All Rights Reserved.

Table of Contents

Foreword	5
Preface	7
Introduction | Questions 1–2	11
Part One: Creation | Questions 3–15	12
Part Two: Fall | Questions 16–22	17
Part Three: Redemption | Questions 23–26	20
Part Four: Restoration | Questions 27–41	22

Foreword

"I, with body and soul, both in life and in death, am not my own, but belong to my faithful savior Jesus Christ." So begins the Heidelberg Catechism. Written by Zacharius Ursinus and published in 1563, The Heidelberg Catechism quickly became a manual for Christian living and religious instruction during the Reformation. A catechism focused on helping Christians lay hold of the deepest truths in the best ways was dearly needed during the tumultuous time of the Reformation.

Today's revolution in theology is not over the doctrine of justification by faith alone, but over sexual identity. Our post-Freudian world maintains without any substantial pushback that sexual identity is the most important truth about a person. Organized under the banner of LGBTQ+, authentic personhood depends on placing yourself under one of these letters, or joyfully and without reservation applauding people who do. The American Medical Association tells us that mental health depends on practicing what you desire, and enthusiastically supporting others who do what feels right in their own eyes is a suicide-prevention strategy. The biblical creation mandate seems a quaint ancient narrative with no binding force when in the United States today there are hundreds of pediatric gender clinics and testosterone is administered to adolescents from Planned Parenthood on a first visit and without parental consent or a therapist's note.

In contrast to the world's anthropology, a biblical anthropology understands that after Adam's transgression (Genesis 3), we, his posterity, have a sin nature that compels each person to love something that God hates. If nothing checks our will, our sinful desires will plunge us headfirst into all manner of spiritual, moral, and sometimes physical danger. No one is exempt from original sin and its consequence. Neither good nor malicious intentions can rewrite God's call for men and women. Scripture is clear that we are responsible for our inborn as well as our actual sins (Psalm 5:5, Romans 1:18, Deuteronomy 27:15, Hebrews 9:27). Taking responsibility for our own sin is hard and necessary, but because of the way that the world, the flesh, and the devil conspire, it is difficult to know where to start.

And this is where Christopher Gordon's *The New Reformation Catechism* offers to the church such a timely and pastoral guide. I have no doubt that this means of discipleship will give glory to God and be used of the Lord to liberate many who are held captive by sexual sin. Twenty-three years ago, when I was in a lesbian relationship and at the same time reading the Bible, I would have greatly benefited from *The New Reformation Catechism on Human Sexuality*. I know that I am not alone in needing this catechism.

May God bless you richly as you grow in Christian liberty. May this catechism help you hold fast to the truth and better understand how the full counsel of God speaks to the godly priority of human sexuality.

Rosaria Butterfield

Preface

The historic creeds and confessions of Protestant churches have served to preserve Christians in the truth of the gospel for centuries. We are deeply indebted to those who took the time to formulate, with great accuracy and clarity, the precious truths of our faith. We are faced with a unique challenge in our times, however, with regard to new movements that are harming the integrity of what we believe.

Of particular interest is how the current sexual revolution has completely overturned what God established at creation as good. This is a unique challenge that has been answered by many helpful writers on the topic. The problem is that not enough Christians are taking the time to read current books that address this issue. Further, few resources are available that are intended to bring families, study groups, and churchgoers together around confessional-like statements that address the challenges of our day.

Creeds and confessions were originally written to provide summary truths of the Christian faith in the face of great theological error. Catechisms in particular provided short, concise summary statements, in question-and-answer format, on some particular doctrine of the Christian faith. These documents are intended to help Christians, especially children and those new to the faith, to have their minds trained in what Scripture teaches on a given point of Christian doctrine. To this day, catechizing is one of the most effective method of preserving Christians from error.

The culture is daily catechizing us and our children in the ideas they want impressed upon minds. It has been to our own demise that Christians have not taken seriously enough the call to combat this vicious assault on our faith through catechizing God's people in his truth. The great need of the moment is a robust recovery in training Christians in the truths of what we confess.

Many of our older confessional statements do not address our current challenges with any amount of specificity. Sadly, due to the fear that any new confession or catechism will challenge the integrity of the confessional statements that we already have, or compromise our present unity, we have avoided the writing of new confessions or catechisms that address current issues.

What is not appreciated, however, is that catechisms in particular were regularly written by Reformed pastors in the sixteenth and seventeenth centuries. Richard Greenham, the great Elizabethan Puritan preacher, second only in influence to William Perkins, wrote a well-known short form of catechizing on the basic principles of the Christian faith. Greenham produced a masterful catechism that helped to provide further clarity on issues that were not specified in ecclesiastically approved Reformed creeds and confessions.

This is precisely the purpose of the present catechism that is being presented to you. There are official, ecclesiastically approved creeds, confessions, and catechisms of the church, that have official authority and serve the churches in the preservation of the truth. This catechism is not an official, ecclesiastical document and does not have the same authority. As a Reformed minister, I have written a pastoral catechism based on the Heidelberg Catechism of 1563 to help Christians have their minds catechized in the truth of biblical human sexuality.

This catechism is intended to be used devotionally around the table, providing an opportunity for parents to talk with their children about these issues. This catechism is also intended to provide opportunities for Bible studies, Sunday school classes, and sermon series for pastors in addressing the current challenges surrounding human sexuality.

I have submitted this catechism to many well-respected scholars and pastors to receive feedback and correction where needed. In particular,

I would like to thank Rosaria Butterfield, Christopher Yuan, R. Scott Clark, W. Robert Godfrey, Carl Trueman, David VanDrunen, Michael Brown, Doug Barnes, Wes Bredenhof, Chad Vegas, Jonathan Cruse, and Jon Payne for their excellent help in producing this catechism.

I hope you will receive this, dear reader, as a humble attempt to help Christians enjoy the creational, sexual ethic that God established from the beginning for our good.

Christopher J. Gordon
Escondido, CA

INTRODUCTION

1. Q. Why is it comforting that we have a new identity in Jesus Christ?

    A. I am being remade into the image of Christ,
    to have a true identity—[1]
    in body and soul,
    throughout the whole course of my life,
    to enjoy God and glorify him forever.[2]

    He redeemed my life with the precious blood of his Son,[3]
    and has delivered me from the lie of Satan in the Garden.[4]
    He also watches over me in such a way
    that he might free me from all sexual impurity
    as the temple of his indwelling;[5]
    in fact, all things must work together
    to remake me into the image of his Son.[6]

    Because I have this new identity,[7]
    Christ, by his Holy Spirit,
    also assures me of God's steadfast love,[8]
    and makes me wholeheartedly willing and ready

---

1 Gen. 1:26-27; Rom. 8:29; 2 Cor. 3:18; Col. 3:10

2 Ps. 146; 1 Cor. 10:31

3 1 Pet. 1:18-19; 1 John 1:7-9; 2:2

4 Gen. 3:4-5; John 8:34-36; Heb. 2:14-15; 1 John 3:1-11

5 1 Cor. 3:16; 1 Cor. 6:15-20

6 Rom. 8:29; 2 Cor. 3:18

7 2 Cor. 5:17

8 Ps. 103:8-10; John 16:25-27

from now on to enjoy true freedom as a new creation.[1]

2. Q. What must I know about human sexuality and my new identity in Christ?

   A. Three things: first, how great my unholy desires and sexual sins are;[2]
second, how I am set free from bondage to my unholy desires and sexual sins;[3]
third, how I am to lead a thankful life of sexual purity in union with Christ.[4]

Part I: CREATION

3. Q. How many sexes did God make at creation?

   A. God made two sexes at creation;
"in the image of God, he created them,
male and female, he created them."[5]

4. Q. What does God require of us in making us in his image?

   A. God requires that we love him
as he created us, male or female,
with all our heart, soul, mind, and strength,
and our neighbor as ourselves.[6]

---

1 John 8:32; Gal. 5:13

2 Ex. 20:14, 17; 2 Sam. 11:2-4; Gal. 5:16; 1 John 2:16

3 2 Sam. 12:13; Ps. 51; 1 Cor. 6:14-7:5; Col. 2:13-15

4 1 Cor. 6:15-20

5 Gen. 1:26-27; 2:18, 21-23; 5:2; Matt. 19:4-5; Mark 10:6-7

6 Lev. 19:18; Deut. 6:5; Matt. 22:37-40

5. Q. Why did God make us male and female in his own image?

   A. That we might use all of the excellent qualities[1]
   with which he made us,[2]
   in true righteousness and holiness,[3]
   in body and soul,[4]
   as male and female,
   for his glory
   as we exercise dominion over the earth.[5]

6. Q. But aren't we able to make a distinction between biological sex and gender in search of our identity?

   A. No. God established a natural order
   in the creation of male and female,
   that is good for us
   as image bearers of God.[6]

   To introduce gender as a new category of personhood,
   separate from the biological category of sex,
   in pursuit of a different sexual identity,
   is unnatural to the creation order,
   and harmful to the purpose for which God made us.[7]

7. Q. But aren't some people born sexually indeterminate?

   A. A small percentage of people are indeed born sexually

---

1 Ps. 8:3-9

2 Ps. 100:3

3 Eph. 4:23-24

4 1 Thess. 5:23

5 Gen. 1:26-27; Ps. 8:3-9

6 Gen. 1:26-31; 9:6; Ps. 8:3-8; James 3:9

7 Gen. 1:31; Ps. 100:3; Rom. 1:21-27

indeterminate due to the fall,
but such are, by definition,
anomalies, and in medicine
anomalies never negate objective categories of personhood.

We may not use the existence of
anomalies to change or redefine
the creational order
that God has established as good.[1]

8. Q. Does God permit us to change our sex?

A. Certainly not.[2]
To reverse how God created us as male or female,
due to fallen, unchosen thoughts and self-perceptions
would be an act of rebellion,[3]
and a gross distortion of God's creative handiwork
in specifically forming us for his own glory.[4]

Further, in the new Jerusalem,
any genital mutilation,
or confusion over sexual orientation identity,
will be restored in our new resurrection bodies.

Therefore, we should not change our sex
since God promises to glorify our bodies,
in everlasting happiness,
as he created us male and female,
in the final resurrection.[5]

---

1 Gen. 1:26-27

2 Deut. 22:5; Deut. 23:1; Ps. 51:3-6

3 Col. 3:5; 1 Thess. 4:5

4 Gen. 2:7, 22; Ps. 100:3

5 Phil. 3:20-21; 1 Cor. 15:35-56; Rev. 21:1-8

9. Q. When was marriage instituted?

> A. The holy bond of marriage
> was instituted by God
> at the very beginning of history in creation.[1]

10. Q. What is marriage?

> A. God created marriage to be a lifelong,
> monogamous covenantal union
> between one man and one woman.[2]

11. Q. Why did God institute marriage?

> A. Six reasons:
>
> First, a husband and wife
> are meant to live together
> in sincere love and holiness,
> helping each other faithfully in all things.[3]
>
> Second, marriage provides husbands and wives
> with a proper setting to enjoy each other
> with the physical and relational desires God gave to them.[4]
>
> Third, by marriage the human race
> is to be continued and increased
> through the institution of the family.[5]

---

1 Questions 9-13 are adapted from the URCNA Statement of Affirmations Regarding Marriage: www.urcna.org/file_retrieve/63166; Gen. 2:18

2 Prov. 2:17; Mark 10:6-9; Eph. 5:25-32

3 Eph. 2:18; Eph. 5:21-25

4 Gen. 2:23; Heb. 13:4

5 Gen. 1:22, 28; 8:17

Fourth, a structure is provided
that enriches society
and contributes to its orderly function.[1]

Fifth, by marriage God advances his kingdom
through the loving devotion of a husband and wife,
as children are nurtured
in the true knowledge and fear of the Lord.[2]

Sixth, marriage is designed to represent
the mystery of Christ and the church
that he loves.[3]

12. Q. Does the Lord permit sexual intimacy outside of marriage?

   A. No. Scripture teaches that marriage
   is the only acceptable context for sexual union.

   Further, God calls us to live decent and chaste lives
   within or outside the holy state of marriage.[4]

13. Q. What is the Christian position on divorce?

   A. Since husbands and wives
   are united by the Lord's hand,
   nothing should separate them in this life.[5]

14. Q. But aren't there any biblical grounds for divorce?

---

1 Gen. 1:26-28

2 Gen. 1:28; Ps. 127:3; Mal. 2:15-16; Eph. 5:22-6:4

3 Eph. 5:25

4 Gen. 2:21-24; Ex. 20:14; 1 Cor. 7:1-2; Eph. 5:3-5; Heb. 13:4

5 Gen. 2:21-14; Matt. 19:6; Mark 10:7-9

A. The Scriptures permit divorce
in the irreconcilable circumstances
of adultery or abandonment.[1]

But these are exceptions
to the general rule not to divorce.

15. Q. Does God permit same-sex marriage?

A. Absolutely not.
God ordained marriage
only between a man and a woman
for life.[2]

Governments do not have the authority
to change marriage
into something contrary
to what God instituted at creation.[3]

Part II: FALL

16. Q. With what lie did Satan tempt our first parents in the garden?

A. Satan lied about the goodness
of God's creation order.

He presented God
as restrictive and oppressive,
and our first parents chose to sin
through the desire to become their own gods

---

[1] Matt. 19:1-9; 1 Cor. 7:10-17

[2] Gen. 2:24; Lev. 18:22; Matt. 19:5; Mark 7:21; Rom. 1:24-32; 1 Cor. 6:9; Eph. 5:31

[3] Acts 5:28-29; Rom. 13:1-2

and define their own way.[1]

17. Q. What happened to our desires in the fall of our first parents, Adam and Eve, in paradise?

A. All the desires of the human heart,
even though they may be unchosen,
have become distorted and fallen
in the sin of our first parents.[2]

These desires cannot be trusted,[3]
since we have a natural tendency to be
led away by various passions.[4]

18. Q. But didn't God create us to be happy in following the desires of our hearts?

A. God made us holy and happy;[5]
we, however,
accepting the lie of the devil,[6]
have robbed ourselves of this happiness
by obeying sinful desires.[7]

19. Q. But isn't there a difference between temptation and the practice of evil desires?

---

1 Gen. 3:1-7; John 8:44; 1 John 2:22

2 Gen. 3:16; Jer. 17:9; 1 John 2:16

3 Rom. 7:14-25

4 2 Tim. 3:6; Gal. 5:24; Eph. 2:3

5 Gen. 1:31; Ps. 8:6-9

6 Gen. 3:6

7 Gen. 3:16-19; Ps. 14; Rom. 3:10-18

A. God requires that we avoid
entering into all forms of temptation.[1]

Temptation is not sin
when it originates outside of us.[2]

Temptation becomes sin
when we entertain and welcome
the sinful desires of our hearts and act upon them.[3]

20. Q. Are we able to make a distinction between entertaining a sinful desire and choosing to live in that desire?

A. God condemns desires that are contrary to his law,
as well as our actual sins.[4]

These contrary desires are sinful
even if they are unchosen,
since they proceed from a corrupt heart.[5]

All impure thoughts and desires,
prior to the conscious act of the will,
are considered sin in God's eyes.[6]

21. Q. What kinds of sinful desires and deeds does God's law condemn?

---

1 Matt. 6:13

2 Gen. 39:6-12; Matt. 4:1-10

3 Gen. 3:6; 4:6-8; 2 Kings 5:20-27

4 Prov. 6:25; 7; Matt. 5:28; 1 Cor. 10:6; Gal. 5:16

5 Matt. 15:19; James 1:15

6 Rom. 2:15-16; 8:5; Eph. 4:17-19; Rev. 2:23

A. Christ teaches us this in summary in Matthew 15:18-20: "But what comes out of the mouth proceeds from the heart, and this defiles a person. For out of the heart come evil thoughts, murder, adultery, sexual immorality, theft, false witness, slander. These are what defile a person."

22. Q. Will God permit our sinful desires to go unpunished?

A. Certainly not.
He is terribly angry with our sinful desires,
as well as our actual sins,
God will punish every idle thought,
careless word,
or wicked action
by a just judgment both now and in eternity.[1]
As the Bible declares,
"For we must all appear before the judgment seat of Christ, so that each one may receive what is due for what he has done in the body, whether good or evil."[2]

Part III: REDEMPTION

23. Q. What has Jesus accomplished for me in the gospel with regard to all forms of sexual sin?

A. Through true faith in the promise of God's Word,[3]
and wholehearted trust in Christ,[4]
by the gospel,
God has freely granted—

---

1 Matt. 12:35-37; Rom. 1:18-32; 2:16; Rev. 20:11-15

2 2 Cor. 5:10

3 John 17:3,17; Heb. 11:1-3; James 2:19

4 Rom. 4:18-21; 5:1; 10:10; Heb. 4:14-16

not only to others but to me also—
the forgiveness of all my sexual trespasses,[1]
canceling all my guilt[2]
and meriting for me eternal righteousness and salvation.[3]

24. Q. How does the truth of the gospel set us free with regard to sexual sin?

A. Since I died, was buried, and have been raised with Christ[4]
through his death and resurrection,
I am set free from slavery to any form of sexual sin.

Christ has broken its dominion over me,[5]
and I now live with a renewed desire[6]
to reckon myself dead to my old way of sexual immorality,[7]
but alive to God in pursuing a sexually pure life for his glory.[8]

25. Q. Since I am no longer my own but have been bought with the precious blood of Christ, what new identity has Christ achieved for me?

A. By faith I am joined to Christ as a new creature,[9]

---

1 Col. 2:13-14; 1 Cor. 6:13-14

2 Col. 2:14; Heb. 2:14

3 Rom. 1:16-17; Heb. 10:10

4 Rom. 6:1-4

5 Rom. 6:5-14

6 Heb. 8:10-12; Col. 3:1-5

7 Rom. 6:21; Eph. 5:1-17

8 Rom. 6:11

9 Eph. 1:7-14

and so I share in his identity.[1]

In my new identity,
I am satisfied in God's love as his adopted child;[2]
I am to think of myself as purchased, accepted, valued, and protected;[3]
and I am to find it a great delight to be remade in the image of Christ
in true righteousness and holiness.[4]

26. Q. Why are all forms of sexual immorality incompatible with my union with Jesus Christ?

    A. Since I have become one with Christ in body and spirit,
any form of sexual immorality
invites that which is profane
into my holy union with Christ.[5]

        Therefore, I am called to be one with Christ
by fleeing all forms of sexual immorality.[6]

Part IV: RESTORATION

27. Q. What does God call us to do when we fall to sexual sin?

    A. When I commit any form of sexual sin—
even the slightest desire or thought

---

1 Gal. 3:28; Eph. 1:9-11; Rom. 8:29; 2 Cor. 5:17

2 Rom. 8:16-17; 9:26; Eph. 2:19; 5:1

3 Rom. 8:32; 2 Thess. 2:16; 1 Pet. 1:18-19

4 Eph. 4:22-24; 1 Pet. 1:8

5 1 Cor. 6:15-20

6 1 Cor. 6:18; 1 Thess. 4:3

contrary to any of God's commandments—
I should confess my sins to him,[1]
eagerly turn away from all sexual sin,[2]
and seek to walk in the newness of life.[3]

28. Q. Is God angry with his children who still struggle in their striving to put away sexual immorality?

A. God is merciful and gracious,
slow to anger,
and abounding in lovingkindness.[4]

When we come to God with a broken and contrite heart,[5]
confessing and turning away from our sins,
God promises to forgive us our sins
and to cleanse us from all unrighteousness.[6]

He has declared,
"a bruised reed he will not break,
and a faintly burning wick he will not quench."[7]

29. Q. What about believers who fight against same-sex attraction but continue to experience shame and guilt for these desires?

A. God, in the gospel of his Son,
has announced that there is no condemnation

---

1 Ps. 1; 32:5; 2 Sam 12:13; 1 John 1:9

2 1 Cor. 6:18; 1 Thess. 4:3

3 Rom. 6:4; 7:6; Col. 3:1-5

4 Ps. 103:1-14

5 Ps. 34:18; 51:17

6 Rom. 4:6-8; 1 John 1:9

7 Isa. 42:3

for those who are in Christ Jesus.[1]
Any unholy desire, even if unchosen,
such as same-sex attraction,
is covered by the blood of Christ.[2]

Believers who continue to struggle
against same-sex attraction,
should trust in God's forgiving mercies,[3]
and with earnest purpose,
by the strength of the Holy Spirit,
strive to live in the newness of life.[4]

Further, the body of Christ
should not avoid or shun
those who struggle against any sexual sin.[5]
Instead, believers, with a spirit of compassion,[6]
should "bear each other's burdens,
and so fulfill the law of Christ."[7]

30. Q. Since we have been delivered from all sexual sin, why should we pursue a life of sexual purity?

    A. Five reasons:

        First, because our sinful desires do not define us
        or constitute our identity

---

1 Rom. 8:1

2 Col. 2:13

3 1 John 1:9

4 Rom. 6:4; Col. 3:1-5

5 2 Sam. 12:1-13; Luke 15:1-2

6 Jude 22; 1 Pet. 3:8

7 Gal. 6:2

as those purchased by the blood of Christ.[1]

Second, because sexual purity
is the will of God for our sanctification,[2]
as we are being renewed
by the power of the Holy Spirit
into the image of God's Son.[3]

Third, by pursuing a life of sexual purity,
we show that we are thankful
to God for his salvation.[4]

Fourth, we also stand as witnesses,
that those living in sexual immorality
might see in us the holy purity that God loves.[5]

Fifth, as we battle against our sinful nature,
the Holy Spirit strengthens our Christian walk
and we give glory to God.[6]

31. Q. What is pornography?

   A. Pornography is sexually explicit material
produced to serve lustful desires of the flesh,
activated through the channel of the eye,[7]
through the looking upon of naked images

---

1 1 Cor. 6:20; 7:23; 1 Pet. 1:17-18

2 1 Thess. 4:3

3 Rom. 8:29; 1 Cor. 3:16; 6:19

4 Rom. 6:13; 12:1-2; 1 Pet. 2:5-10

5 Matt. 5:14-16; Rom. 14:17-19; 1 Pet. 2:12; 3:1-2

6 1 Cor. 10:31; Gal. 5:17

7 Job 31:1; 1 John 2:16

of males and females
for the purpose of sexual arousal.[1]

32. Q. Why is pornography so destructive?

   A. Because the use of such images
   ruins the sexual intimacy intended for marriage,[2]
   supports idolatry in the worship of the creature,[3]
   dehumanizes men and women promoting abuse,
   especially of women,[4]
   advances other forms of sexual impurity,[5]
   creates idleness in society to the harm of our neighbors,[6]
   and degrades the mind into darkness.[7]

33. Q. Can those be saved who do not turn to God from their unholy desires and unrepentant of their sexual ways?

   A. By no means.
   Scripture tells us that
   no sexually immoral person,
   no adulterer,
   no fornicator,
   no homosexual,
   no abuser of women,
   or the like

---

1 Matt. 5:28; 1 Cor. 7:9

2 Eph. 5:25; Heb. 13:4

3 Rom. 1:24-25

4 Gen. 1:26-27

5 Rom. 1:18-27; James 1:14-15; 2 Pet. 2:14

6 2 Thess. 3:6-12

7 Rom. 1:28-32; Eph. 4:18-19

will inherit the kingdom of God.[1]

34. Q. What is involved in genuine repentance of all sexual sin?

   A. Two things:

   The dying-away of the old self,
   by hating all forms of sexual immorality
   and fleeing from it;[2]

   And the rising-to-life of the new self,
   by finding great joy in leading a sexually pure life
   and, if married, by properly loving our spouses.[3]

35. Q. How should husbands seek to love and honor their wives?

   A. Husbands should demonstrate sincere love to their wives,
   in reverence for Christ,[4]
   through the exercise of:
   loyalty, kindness, understanding, tenderness, self-control,
   sexual purity,
   by all means avoiding
   verbal, emotional, and physical abuse
   or controlling behavior,
   and by providing godly leadership.[5]

   Men ought to be a good example to their wives

---

[1] 1 Cor. 6:9-10; Gal. 5:19-21; Eph. 5:1-20; 1 John 3:14

[2] 2 Cor. 5:17; Eph. 4:22-24; Col. 3:5-10; 1 Cor. 6:15-20

[3] Ps. 51:8, 12; Isa. 57:15; Rom. 6:1-11; Eph. 5:22-33

[4] Eph. 5:21

[5] Gal. 5:22-26; Eph. 5:25-33; Col. 3:19; 1 Pet. 3:7

of the love that Christ has for his church.[1]

36. Q. How should wives seek to love and honor their husbands?

    A. Wives should demonstrate sincere love to their husbands,
in reverence for Christ,[2]
through the exercise of:
respect, patience, honor, encouragement, self-denial, contentment
and by finding delight in godly submission that pleases the Lord.[3]

    Women ought to be a good example to their husbands
of the responsive love that the church has for Christ.[4]

37. Q. How should singles honor the Lord in the situation that God has called them?

    A. Singles who desire marriage
are called to contentment and prayer,[5]
trusting the Lord in every circumstance[6]
as he knows best for us,
yet realizing that only Christ makes us fulfilled,
and that ultimate joy is found in Christ whether as single or married.[7]

---

1 Eph. 5:25; Col. 3:19

2 Eph. 5:21

3 Prov. 31:10-31; Eph. 5:22-24; Titus 2:1-5; 1 Pet. 3:1-4

4 Eph. 5:28-30

5 Phil. 4:11

6 Prov. 3:5-7

7 Prov. 18:22

> Singles who do not desire marriage,
> are called to holiness in body and spirit,[1]
> in the special opportunities they have
> to give "undivided devotion to the Lord,"[2]
> yet, should remain open to God's will to provide a spouse
> and change one's desire for marriage.

38. Q. How should the family be maintained to the glory of God?

> A. By making Christ the center of our homes through:
> love, humility, and patience toward one another;[3]
> godly discipline,[4]
> the regular reading of the Scriptures,[5]
> heartfelt prayer,[6]
> removing all things spiritually harmful from our homes,[7]
> and making Lord's Day worship a priority together.[8]

39. Q. What is God's will for parents in training children in proper sexuality?

> A. Three things:
>
> First, that parents model before their children
> a loving relationship,
> and also hold marriage in honor

---

1 1 Cor. 7:6-9

2 1 Cor. 7:35

3 Eph. 4:25-32

4 Eph. 6:1-4

5 Deut. 6:6-9; Col. 3:16; 1 Tim. 4:13

6 1 Thess. 5:17

7 Josh. 24:15; 2 Kings 23-24; Eph. 4:31

8 Heb. 10:25

as it was designed by God.[1]

Second, that parents speak to their children
appropriately and sufficiently
about biblical sexuality,
and proper sexual conduct,
as designed for marriage;[2]
realizing that our children are facing
daily misinformation on sexuality.

Third, that parents guard their children from
all forms of sexual immorality and pornography,[3]
and overseeing the use of technology, social media,
and other mediums that promote,
through cultural peer pressure,
a different sexual ethic[4]
than what God made as good in creation.[5]

40. Q. What is God's will for young adults in honoring their parents in sexual conduct?

A. Three things:

First, that young adults honor their parents by
maintaining sexual purity and chastity.[6]

Second, that young adults refrain

---

1 Eph. 5:21-25

2 Prov. 5; 7; 22:6, 15; Heb. 13:4

3 Job 31:1

4 1 Thess. 4:3

5 Deut. 6:6-9

6 Ex. 22:16; 1 Cor. 6:18-20; 7; Heb. 13:4

from pushing upon their parents
and adopting the ungodly sexual norms
of the culture.[1]

Third, that young adults take delight in the Lord
and in their identity in Christ as singles,
waiting patiently for the spouse
that God prepares for them.[2]

41. Q. How do we love those who live in sexual sin?

A. We should not avoid or shun
those who are mastered by sexual sin.[3]
Instead, we should speak the truth in love[4]
about sexual sin, repentance, and faith in Christ;
give witness to the deliverance God gave us
from our own sins;[5]
and perform acts of kindness.[6]
By our godly living,
we should seek to win over our neighbors to Christ.[7]

---

1 Deut. 21:18-21; Prov. 29:15; 30:17; Col. 3:20; 1 Tim. 3:1-4

2 Gen. 2:22-23; Prov. 18:22

3 Luke 15:1-2; Matt. 9:13

4 Eph. 4:15

5 Mark 5:19; 1 Pet. 3:15

6 Matt. 5:43-48; Luke 14:12-14; Rom. 12:13; Heb 13:16; 1 Pet. 4:9

7 Matt. 5:14-16; Rom. 14:17-19; 1 Pet. 2:12; 3:1-2

GOSPEL REFORMATION NETWORK

To cultivate healthy Reformed churches in the Presbyterian Church in America.

Vision & Distinctives

1. Biblical Fidelity & Confessional Integrity
An unyielding commitment to the inspiration, inerrancy, authority, sufficiency, and efficacy of Scripture for faith and practice, along with a resolute adherence to the Westminster Standards (Isa. 55:10-11; 2 Tim. 3:16-17; Titus 1:9; 2 Pet. 1:21; Rom. 10:17; Jude 3; Heb. 10:23).

2. Gospel-Driven & Christ-Exalting Ministry
A sincere passion to proclaim the gospel of grace, always with the aim of exalting Christ in the hearts, minds, and affections of God's people (1 Cor. 1:23; 2:2; Eph. 3:8; John 21:15-19; Phil. 1:21; 3:8).

3. Earnest Prayer & Expository Preaching
A resolve to practice fervent prayer in the closet and from the pulpit, along with an unbending dedication to expository preaching that informs the mind, transforms the heart, and stirs the affections (Matt. 6:5-13; 1 Thess. 5:17; Acts 2:42; Eph. 1:15-23; Acts 2:14-36, 42; 12:5; 20:27; Rom. 10:14-15; 2 Tim. 4:1-5).

4. Intentional Evangelism & Personal Discipleship
A purposeful commitment to bold evangelism, coupled with a dedication to the old paths of serious, deliberate, faith-maturing discipleship (Luke 9:1-6; Acts 7:1-60; 8:26-40; Matt. 28:19; Luke 9:23-24; Col. 1:28-29).

5. Godly Leadership & Presbyterian Polity
A sincere devotion to personal piety among church leadership, coupled with a strong adherence to biblical Presbyterianism (Acts 20:28; 1 Tim. 4:12; 1 Pet. 5:1-4; Acts 15:1-21; 1 Tim. 3:1-7; Titus 1:5-9).

6. Reformed Worship & Vibrant Community
A joyful commitment to, and humble confidence in, the ordinary means of grace in Lord's Day worship, coupled with the nurture of loving Christian fellowship (Ex. 20:1-11; Ps. 100; Acts 2:42-47; 20:7; Rom. 12:10; 1 Cor. 11:17-34; 12:12-31; John 13:34; WCF XXI; WLC Q. 153-196).

7. Missional Clarity & Church Multiplication
A fervent and undistracted commitment to make disciples of all nations through the preaching of the gospel and the planting and strengthening of biblical churches (Matt. 28:16-20; Acts 14:7, 21-23; 15:35; Rom. 10:14-17; Titus 1:5-9).